THE HISTORY OF
THE ENGLISH LANGUAGE

The time: from about 5000 BC to the twenty-first century and beyond. The place: a distant corner of southern Russia, the railways of the United States, the Caribbean farms where sugar is grown, an airport in Japan, the chat rooms of the Internet – and almost every place in the world today. The machines: the printing press, TV, the mobile phone, the computer. The people: Celtic travellers, Viking invaders, French landowners, kings, business people, writers, singers, and millions of people like you or me.

Bring them all together, and you have the history of the English language, with its changing grammar, spelling, pronunciation, and vocabulary. It's a story without an end, that involves millions of people. Some helped to shape the language of the past, and others are making the English of the future. And one of those people is you . . .

OXFORD BOOKWORMS LIBRARY

Factfiles

The History of the English Language

Stage 4 (1400 headwords)

Factfiles Series Editor: Christine Lindop

BRIGIT VINEY

The History of
the English Language

OXFORD UNIVERSITY PRESS

OXFORD
UNIVERSITY PRESS

Great Clarendon Street, Oxford OX2 6DP

Oxford University Press is a department of the University of Oxford.
It furthers the University's objective of excellence in research, scholarship,
and education by publishing worldwide in

Oxford New York

Auckland Cape Town Dar es Salaam Hong Kong Karachi
Kuala Lumpur Madrid Melbourne Mexico City Nairobi
New Delhi Shanghai Taipei Toronto

With offices in

Argentina Austria Brazil Chile Czech Republic France Greece
Guatemala Hungary Italy Japan Poland Portugal Singapore
South Korea Switzerland Thailand Turkey Ukraine Vietnam

OXFORD and OXFORD ENGLISH are registered trade marks of
Oxford University Press in the UK and in certain other countries

ISBN: 978 0 19 423397 2

A complete recording of this Bookworms edition of *The History of
the English Language* is available.

Printed in China

Word count (main text): 16753

For more information on the Oxford Bookworms Library,
visit www.oup.com/elt/bookworms

ACKNOWLEDGEMENTS
Illustrations pp 4, 7 by: Gareth Riddiford
The publishers would like to thank the following for permission to reproduce the following images:
Alamy Images pp viii (Stock Connection Blue), 8 (Viking rune stone/Stefan Sollfors),
32 (The Globe theatre/Vehbi Koca), 45 (DNA/Phototake Inc.), 45 (iPod/D.Hurst),
52 (Landing of the Pilgrims/Visual Arts Library, London),
52 (Dutch purchase of Manhattan Island/North Wind Picture Archives),
52 (slave trade/Visual Arts Library, London), 64 (Stock AB), 72 (Eddie Gerald);
The Art Archive pp 15 (The British Library, London), 20 (Bibliotheque Municipale Valenciennes/
Dagli Orti, *Teacher*); The Bridgeman Art Library pp 17 (Musee de la Tapisserie,
Bayeux France), 23 (Musee Conde, Chantilly, France), 29 (Private Collection, *Aesop's Fables*),
36 (Phillip Mould, Historical Portraits Ltd, London, Swift), 39 (Private Collection, Johnson), 51;
Corbis pp 30 (Bob Krist), 49 (Charles Gullung/zefa), 53 (Italian immigrants/Bettmann),
53 (children on boat/Bettmann), 62 (Esther Anderson), 66 (Karl Weatherly),
71 (Michael S.Yamashita); D.C Thomson & Co.Ltd p 59 (Oor Wullie); Heritage Image
Partnership Limited p 12 (Lindisfarne Gospels, c700/The British Library/
Heritage-Images); The New York Public Library p 53 (German immigrants, Ellis Island, 1926/
Lewis W. Hine); North Wind Picture Archive p 54 (transcontinental railroad/
North Wind); OUP Archives 34, 40, 46; Rex Features p 58.

CONTENTS

WELCOM
Bienvenue
Chào Mừng
добро пожаловать
어서오세요
Bienvenido
歡迎

1   A world language

The English language is spoken today in parts of Europe, the Americas, Asia, Africa, Australia, New Zealand, and in some of the islands of the Atlantic, Indian, and Pacific Oceans. It is spoken as a first language by 370 to 400 million people. It is also used as a second language by a similar number of people, and as a foreign language by hundreds of millions more. English is probably used in some way by about a quarter of all the people in the world. Because so many people, in so many places, speak or use English, it is often called a 'world language'.

Who uses English, and why is it such a widely spoken language? In countries like Britain and the US, English is the first language of most people: in other words, it is the first language people learn as children and they communicate in English all the time. In other countries, like India, Kenya, Singapore, and Papua New Guinea, large numbers of people use English as a second language. They have their own first language, but because English is one of the official languages, they use it in education, business, government, radio, and television. Finally, in many countries English is taught in schools as a foreign language, but it is not an official language.

English is also used for many different kinds of international communication. People in science, medicine, and business often communicate in English. English is the language of much of the world's pop music and films. The 'languages' of international sea and air traffic control, known as 'Seaspeak' and 'Airspeak', use English. They use a small number of

English words and sentences to make communication clearer and simpler. (For example, in Seaspeak instead of saying 'Sorry, what was that?' or 'What did you say?' you say 'Say again'.) Much of the world's news is reported in English on television, the radio, the Internet, or in newspapers.

The spread of English around the world began with the British settlement of North America, the Caribbean, Australia, and Asia in the seventeenth and eighteenth centuries. It continued in the nineteenth century when the British controlled parts of Africa and the South Pacific. English also became important internationally because in the nineteenth century Britain was the most important industrial nation in the world. Many new machines came from Britain, so people had to learn English in order to learn how to use them.

In the twentieth century, the use of English spread with the growth in international business. Air travel developed, making more international business possible. Faster ways of international communication, like the telephone and more recently the computer, became more widely used. Many people wanted to do business with American companies because the US was rich, and in order to do this they had to speak English. When international companies and organizations developed, English was often chosen as the working language. For example, English is the working language of the European Central Bank, although the bank is in Germany. In Asia and the Pacific, nine out of ten international organizations work only in English.

English is important not because it has more first-language speakers than other languages (Chinese has more) but because it is used extremely widely. Will this situation continue? This is an interesting question, but first let us look at how English began.

2 The beginnings of English

Our understanding of the history of English began at the end of the eighteenth century when Sir William Jones, a British judge who lived in India, began to study Sanskrit. This is a very old language of India, and at the time was used in Indian law. Like others before him, Jones noticed many similarities between Sanskrit, Latin, Greek, and other European languages. For example:

SANSKRIT	LATIN	GREEK	ENGLISH
pitr	pater	pater	father
matar	mater	matr	mother
asti	est	esti	is
trayah	tres	treis	three
sapta	septem	hepta	seven

People had thought that Latin, Greek, and all European languages came from Sanskrit, but Jones disagreed. In 1786 he wrote that Sanskrit, Greek, and Latin all came from a 'common source', which had perhaps disappeared. There was a lot of interest in his idea and other people began to study these three languages. Their work proved that Jones was right. We now know that Sanskrit, Greek, Latin, English, and many other languages all belong to one enormous 'family' of languages called the Indo-European family.

Jones's 'common source' from which all these languages developed is now known as Proto-Indo-European. It is

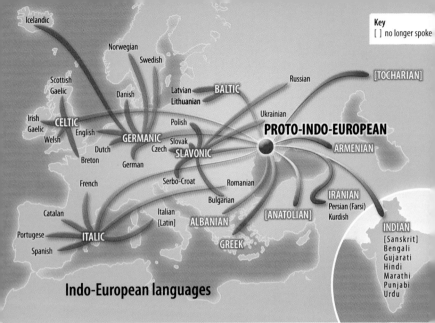

Indo-European languages

thought that a group of people called the Kurgans spoke this language, or dialects of it, and lived in what is now southern Russia from some time after 5000 BC. In about 3500 BC the Kurgans probably began to spread west across Europe and east across Asia. As groups of Kurgans travelled further and further away from each other, they began to develop stronger differences in their dialects. With the passing of time, these dialects became different languages. When some of them (the Greek, Anatolian, and Indo-Iranian languages) appear in written form in about 2000 to 1000 BC they are clearly separate languages.

Similarities between some languages as they are spoken today suggest that they probably come from Proto-Indo-European. For example, there are similar words in European and Indo-Iranian languages for people in the family (*mother*, *father*), animals (*dog*, *sheep*, *horse*), parts of the body (*eye*, *ear*), the weather (*rain*, *snow*), and for weapons. These similarities allow us to imagine something of the life of the Kurgans: they worked on the land some of the time, made clothes from wool, and used wheels.

More than 2 billion people speak an Indo-European language as their first language. The speaker of Hindi in India, the speaker of Portuguese in Brazil, and the speaker of English in Australia all express themselves in Indo-European languages.

The Celts were the first group of Indo-European speakers to move across Europe. Towards the end of the fifth century BC they began to leave their homeland north of the Alps in central Europe. They went to the Black Sea, Turkey, south-west Spain and central Italy, the whole of Britain, and Ireland. As they travelled, different dialects of their language developed. The Celts who settled in Turkey spoke Galatian, those in Spain spoke Celtiberian, and those in France, Italy, and northern Europe spoke Gaulish. The Celts who went to Ireland and later Scotland spoke Goidelic (Gaelic) and those who went to southern England and Wales spoke Brythonic (or British).

Unfortunately for the Celts in Britain, other people wanted to take advantage of the island's good farming land and valuable metals. In AD 43 the Romans invaded Britain. They remained there for almost four hundred years, and almost all of what is now England came under their control. (They never went very far into Wales or Scotland.) They introduced a new way of life and a new language – Latin. British Celts in the upper classes and the towns became used to life with laws and police, roads, baths, and theatres. Some learnt to speak and write Latin. However, a new language did not develop from Latin in Britain as French did in Gaul and Spanish did in Spain.

From the middle of the third century AD, the Romans grew weaker and weaker as the Germanic peoples of northern Europe invaded more and more Roman lands. In AD 410 the Romans finally left Britain. Without the Roman army to guard it, the country was in danger from other invaders.

In AD 449, people from Jutland in modern Denmark – the Jutes – arrived in southern Britain and the Angles – also from Denmark – came and settled in eastern Britain. In 477 the Saxons, from what is now Germany, came and settled in southern and south-eastern Britain. These three Germanic peoples were very different from the Romans. The Romans had governed the British Celts, but they had not taken their lands. The Jutes, Angles, and Saxons came in larger numbers and they settled on the lands belonging to the British Celts. Some of the British Celts left and went north, some went west into Wales and Cornwall, and others went over the sea to Brittany, in what is now northern France.

The Jutes stayed in Kent, in the south-east of Britain, but the Angles moved north and the Saxons went south-west. They slowly organized themselves into seven kingdoms in what is now England and south-east Scotland. In the seventh century the kingdom of Northumbria, in the north, was very strong and a great centre of learning. In the eighth century Mercia, in the centre, became the most important kingdom, and in the ninth century Wessex, in the south and south-west, became the strongest kingdom.

The invaders called the British Celts **wealas** meaning *foreigners*. Later this meant both *Celts* and *servants*. From **wealas** comes the Modern English word *Welsh*. The British Celts called all the invaders 'Saxons' at first, but in the sixth century the word **Angli** was used to mean the whole group of invaders. Later **Angli** became **Engle**. Today we call them 'Anglo-Saxons'. From the various Germanic dialects used by these people, English developed.

3 Old English

Old English is the language that was spoken from the middle of the fifth century to the middle of the twelfth century in what is now England and southern Scotland. During this time the language changed and took in words from other languages.

There were four main dialects of Old English: West Saxon (in the south and south-west), Kentish (in the south-east), Mercian (in the centre and east), and Northumbrian (in the north). The dialects had small differences of grammar, vocabulary, and pronunciation.

Unlike other invaders, the Anglo-Saxons kept their own language and did not learn the language of the British Celts. They did not take many Celtic words into their dialects either; only about twenty Celtic words are found in Old English. The Anglo-Saxons borrowed some

The main Old English dialects

Northumbrian

Mercian

Kentish

West Saxon

Celtic words for parts of the countryside which were new to them: for example, the words *crag* and *tor* meaning *a high rock*, and *cumb* for *a deep valley*. The names of some English cities, *London* and *Leeds* for example, are Celtic, and the word **dubris**, which meant *water,* became *Dover*. Different Celtic words for *river* or *water* survive in the river names *Avon*, *Esk*, and *Ouse*, and *Thames* is also Celtic, meaning *dark river*. However, there are very few ordinary Celtic words in Old English, and no one is really sure of the reason for this.

Old English in the fifth and sixth centuries did have some words that were not Germanic. These were Latin words, which the Anglo-Saxons had borrowed from the Romans before invading Britain. But there were not many – only about fifty. Some examples are **strǣt** (*street*), **weall** (*wall*), and **wīn** (*wine*).

Runes cut into stone

Most Anglo-Saxons could not read or write, but those who could write used runes. These were letters which had been used by the Germanic peoples since about the third century AD. They were cut into stone or weapons and were often used to say that someone had made or owned something.

The arrival of Augustine and about forty monks in 597 brought changes to Anglo-Saxon life in Britain and to Old English. They had come from Rome to teach the Anglo-Saxons about Christianity. Although Christianity was not new in Britain, this was the first organized attempt to make the people of Britain Christians. Augustine and the monks were welcomed in Canterbury in the south-east by King Aethelbert of Kent and Queen Bertha, who was a Christian. In the following century these monks and others took Christianity over the south of the country. In the north, people learnt about Christianity from the Irish monk Aidan, who arrived there in 635. By the end of the seventh century all the Anglo-Saxon kingdoms were Christian.

The monks built churches and taught poetry, Greek, and Latin as well as Christianity. As a result, a number of Latin words entered Old English: about 450 appear in Old English literature. Some were about the life of the Church: for example, **munuc** (*monk*) and **scōl** (*school*). Others were words for things in the house: **fenester** (*window*) and **cest** (*chest*). Some verbs from Latin were **spendan** (*to spend*), **sealtian** (*to dance*), and **tyrnan** (*to turn*).

At first the monks wrote only in Latin, but then they began to write in Old English. This was unusual: people in other northern European countries did not begin writing in their own languages until much later. Learning spread and flowered among the Anglo-Saxons, and by the eighth century England was a centre of learning in western Europe.

Old English was usually written with these letters:

a, æ, b, c, d, e, f, ʒ, h, i, l, m, n, o, p, r, s, t, þ, ð, u, ƿ, y.

Most of these were Roman, but some were not. 'Thorn' þ and 'wynn' ƿ were runes. 'Thorn' þ and 'eth' ð were used for the sounds /θ/ and /ð/. Both were used for both sounds. ð was perhaps an Irish letter. 'Wynn' ƿ was used instead of *w*, and 'yogh' ʒ instead of *g*. The letters *k* and *x* were also used occasionally. There were no capital letters.

Writers usually chose their own spellings of words, and they tried to show in the spelling how a word was pronounced. All the letters in a word were pronounced. For example the letter *h* in **hring** (*ring*) was pronounced. The pronunciation of the same word varied from one dialect to another, so there were different spellings of the same word.

The vocabulary of Old English was almost completely Germanic. Much of it – about 85 per cent – has disappeared from Modern English and has been replaced with words from Latin or French. However, many of the words in Modern English that are most often used come from Old English. A few examples are: *the*, *and*, *can*, and *get*. Other words in Modern English which come from Old English are for very basic things and ideas. Some examples are: **mann** (*person*), **cild** (*child*), **hūs** (*house*), **etan** (*eat*), **slǣpan** (*sleep*).

Other words which survive from Old English are names of places. The Anglo-Saxons used **ford** for *a place where a river can be crossed*, **ham** for *village*, **ton** for *farm* or *village*, and **wic** for *house* or *village*. These words survive in many names, for example, *Oxford*, *Birmingham*, *Brighton*, *Warwick*.

Some Modern English names for the days of the week come from the names of Anglo-Saxon gods and goddesses. Tuesday is named after **Tīw**, Wednesday after **Wōden** (both gods of war), Thursday after **Thunor** (god of thunder), and Friday after **Frīg** (goddess of love).

Like other Indo-European languages, Old English made new words by putting two other words together. For example: **bōccrᴂft**, *book-skill*, meant *literature*; **sunnandᴂg**, *sun's day*, meant *Sunday*. Poets often did this to make beautiful descriptions; one expression for *body* was *bone-house* and one for *the sea* was *the water's back*.

Old English also made new words by adding letters before

or after the main word. For example: **gān** (*to go*) became **ingān** (*to go in*), **upgān** (*to go up*), and **ūtgān** (*to go out*). The word **blōd** (*blood*) became **blōdig** (*bloody*), and **blind** became **blindlīce** (*blindly*).

The words in a sentence in Old English often appeared in a different order from those in Modern English. In Modern English, *the girl helped the boy* and *the boy helped the girl* have different meanings which we understand from the word order. In Old English people understood the meaning of a sentence from the endings of each word, and these endings changed to show the job that each word did in the sentence.

Nouns also changed their endings for the plural: for example, **guma** (*man*) became **guman**, **stān** (*stone*) became **stānas**, and **giefu** (*gift*) became **giefa**. Nouns had three genders, and adjectives and articles changed with the gender of the noun. However, many of the possible changes to words did not happen in practice.

There were more personal pronouns than in Modern English. For example, there was **hine** (*him*), **him** (*to him*), **hī** (*her*) and **hire** (*to her*). **Him** also meant *to it* and *to them*. There were also the pronouns **wit** meaning *we two* and **git** meaning *you two*.

Verb endings changed, too. The past tense of most verbs was made by changing a vowel in the present tense, so *sing* changed to *sang*, for example. In Old English there were about twice as many of these irregular verbs as there are today. The past tense of regular verbs was made by adding the endings -*de*, -*ede*, or -*ode*. For example, the past tense of **libban** (*to live*) was **lifde**, the past tense of **cnyssan** (*to push*) was **cnysede**, and the past tense of **lufian** (*to love*) was **lufode**.

In the eighth century Britain was visited by the Vikings,

or 'Danes' as the Anglo-Saxons called them. From 787 they came in many small groups from Denmark and Norway and stole gold and silver from towns and churches on the north coast. In 793 and 794 they destroyed Lindisfarne and Jarrow, two very important Christian centres of learning in the north-east of England. In 850 a large Viking army took London and Canterbury, and so a war began which continued until 878. Then King Alfred (the Anglo-Saxon

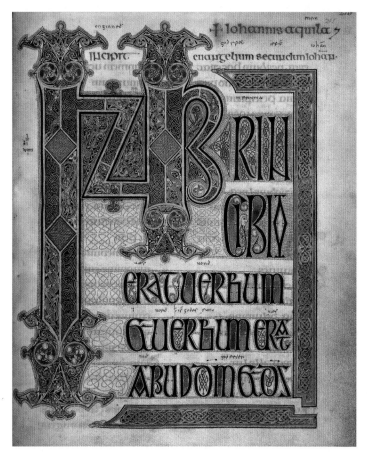

Early writings from Lindisfarne

king of Wessex from 871 to 899) won an important battle, and made an agreement with the Vikings to separate England into two parts. After that, the northern and eastern part, known as the Danelaw, was controlled by the Vikings, and the rest of England was controlled by King Alfred.

In order to bring back the centres of learning that had been destroyed, King Alfred decided to make English, not Latin, the language of education and literature. So at the age of forty he learnt Latin and began translating books into Old English. He described his plan in these words:

> **Therefore it seems better to me . . . that we should also translate certain books which are most necessary for all men to know into the language that we can all understand, and also arrange it . . . so that all the youth of free men now among the English people . . . are able to read English writing well.**

Later he had other books translated into Old English. One of these was *Historia Ecclesiastica Gentis Anglorum* (*The History of the English Church and People*), which had been written in about 731 by a monk in Northumbria called Bede. This is the most important source of information about early English history that we have. In the translation, and in other early English writings, we begin to see the word **Englisc** (*English*) used to describe the people and the language.

King Alfred also started a history of England in English: *The Anglo-Saxon Chronicle*. This was written by monks in different parts of the country. It described what had happened in the past in England, and also what happened every year at the time of writing. It was the first chronicle in Europe that was not written in Latin.

Most of the Old English works that have survived were

written after King Alfred's death. One of the greatest writers was a monk from Wessex called Ælfric (955–1010). He wrote many Christian works and a guide for young monks called *Colloquy*. This was written in Latin as a conversation between a teacher and a student, and it is important for two reasons. It tells us a lot about the daily life of monks and ordinary people, and it also tells us a lot about Old English, because in one copy someone has written the Old English words above the Latin words.

The greatest piece of literature in Old English that has survived is a poem of about 3,000 lines called *Beowulf*. This was probably made in the middle of the eighth century, although it was not actually written down until about two hundred and fifty years later. It tells the story of a brave man from Scandinavia called Beowulf. He fights and kills a terrible animal called Grendel, and then kills Grendel's mother, who is just as terrible. It is a poem about life and death, bravery and defeat, war and peace.

Here is a short piece from it in which Beowulf describes his fight with Grendel ('the devil'):

> . . . wæs tō fore-mihtig
> fēond on feþe. Hwæþere hē his folme forlēt
> tō līf-wraþe lāst weardian,
> earm ond eaxle . . .
>
> > . . . *the devil pulled free*
> > *with enormous force. But, in order to save*
> > *his life, he left behind his hand,*
> > *his arm and his shoulder* . . .

In the Danelaw the Vikings and the English were able to communicate quite well, because their two languages, Old Norse and Old English, were both Germanic. One effect of this was that Old English became simpler. Many of the different word endings disappeared. Plural endings became simpler as the -*s* ending was more widely used, and many verbs which used to change their vowel to make the past tense now began to take the -*de* ending instead.

Another result was that thousands of words from Old Norse (ON) entered Old English (OE). Between four and five hundred remain in use today, with hundreds more in the dialects of northern England and Scotland. We can see

The first page of *Beowulf*

that the speakers of the two languages lived together closely, because the Old Norse words that came into Old English are words from everyday life – words for the house (*window*), parts of the body (*leg, neck*), and common verbs (*get, take, want*). There are also many words beginning with *sk-* like *skin, skirt,* and *sky.* Others are: *bag, die, egg, husband, same.* Some Old Norse words replaced Old English words; for example **syster** (ON) replaced **sweostor** (OE) for *sister.* In some cases, both the Old Norse and Old English words for the same idea were used. For example, there was *wish* (OE) and *want* (ON), and *sick* (OE) and *ill* (ON).

The Old Norse word *are* replaced the Old English **sindon** and the Old Norse verb ending -*s* for the third person singular in the present tense began to be used. The Old Norse *they, their,* and *them* slowly replaced the Old English **hī, hire,** and **hem** in the following centuries.

The Vikings also left their mark on place names. More than 1,500 places in northern England have Scandinavian names. Over 600 end in -*by*, which means *farm* or *town* (for example, *Whitby*). Others end in -*thorp(e)* (*small village*), and -*toft* (*piece of land*); for example, *Scunthorpe* and *Blacktoft.* Modern family names that end in -*son,* like *Johnson* and *Davidson,* also come from the Vikings.

Battles between the Vikings and the English continued in the tenth century. From 1016 to 1041 England had Danish kings, who were then followed by an English king, Edward. When Edward died in 1066, Harold, the leader of Wessex, was chosen to be the next king. However, William, one of Edward's cousins, said that Edward had promised that *he* would become king of England. William was the leader of Normandy in northern France. He decided to take an army to England and fight Harold.

4 The Normans in England

At the Battle of Hastings, on 14 October 1066, King Harold was killed and his army was defeated by the Normans. On Christmas Day 1066 William was made king of England in London, and over the next four years he completed his conquest of England and Wales. This conquest had a very great effect on the development of the English language.

William had large stone castles built, from which Norman soldiers controlled the towns and countryside. He took very large areas of land from rich English families and gave them to his Norman followers. Each of these new landowners had his own group of soldiers, and each gave land to his own followers, so there was usually one Norman family in each English village. Normans worked in the government and business and controlled the Church.

Norman French immediately became the language of the

The Battle of Hastings

governing classes and remained so for the next two hundred years. French and Latin were used in government, the Church, the law, and literature. Very little was written in English, although English monks continued writing *The Anglo-Saxon Chronicle* until 1154. English was still spoken, however, in its different regional dialects.

The use of French continued in England during the twelfth century, partly because many of the Norman kings and landowners also had land in Normandy and other parts of France and they spent a lot of time there. French was not spoken only by people of Norman or French blood. It was also spoken by English people who wanted to be important.

Slowly, however, English became more widely used by the Normans. Many of the Normans married English women, so they and their children spoke English. In 1177, one English writer reported that with 'free men' it was impossible to know who was English and who was Norman.

In 1204 King John of England lost Normandy to the king of France, and during the next fifty years all the great landowning families in England had to give away their lands in France. They became less involved with France and began to feel that England was their country.

The upper classes continued to speak French as a second language, and it was still used in government and the law. However, French started to become less important socially in England, partly because the Norman French spoken in England was not considered 'good' by speakers of Parisian French in France. The upper classes began to feel prouder of their English than of their French.

Most ordinary people could not speak French at all. At the end of the thirteenth century, one poet wrote:

Lewede men cune Ffrensch non
Among an hondryd vnneþis on.

> *Common men know no French*
> *Among a hundred scarcely one.*

Ordinary people did not need to learn French, and probably did not want to. It was the language of the Normans, who had destroyed many English towns and villages. English was the language of the country, and people were proud of it and of their history. A poet in around 1300 wrote in his introduction to the poem *Cursor Mundi*:

Þis ilk bok es translate
Into Inglis tong to rede
For the love of Inglis lede,
Inglis lede of Ingland,
For the commun at understand.

> *This book is translated*
> *Into the English language*
> *For the love of the English people,*
> *English people of England,*
> *And for the common people to understand.*

The continuing bad feeling between England and France resulted in the Hundred Years War (1337–1453). During this time national feeling grew and the English language was seen more and more as an important part of being English.

Between 1348 and 1375 England was hit several times by the illness known as the Black Death and almost a third of the people in England died. Many churchmen, monks, and school teachers died and were replaced by less educated men who spoke only English. There were fewer ordinary working people, so they could ask for better conditions

A court of law in London

from the landowners. Many left the land and went to work for more money in the towns. As ordinary people became more important, their language – English – became more important too. It was used more and more in government, as fewer and fewer people could understand French. In 1362, English was used for the first time at the opening of Parliament.

When Henry the Fourth became king in 1399, England had its first English-speaking king since 1066. In the following century English took the place of French in the home, in education, and in government. It also became the language of written communication so that after 1450 most letters were in English, not Latin.

English had survived – but it had changed.

5   Middle English

In the four centuries that followed the Norman Conquest, the English language changed more than in any other time in its history. Thousands of words from French came into the language, and many Old English ones left it. At the same time the language changed grammatically, mainly by becoming simpler. The English used in this time is called Middle English.

One way the grammar grew simpler was by losing some of the different endings for nouns, adjectives, and pronouns. For example, by the fifteenth century the plural noun ending *-(e)s* was accepted everywhere in England, although some plurals with *-en* survived (*children* is one of them). Other noun endings which have survived are the *'s* (*the boy's book*) and the *s'* (*the boys' books*). Adjectives and nouns also lost their grammatical gender, and *the* became the only form of the definite article.

The main change to verbs was to the past tense. Some of the Old English verbs began to end in *-ed*. For example, the past tense of *climb* was **clomb**, but the word *climbed* also began to appear in the thirteenth century. In the fourteenth century, most of the thousands of verbs which had entered the language from French also formed the past tense with *-ed*. Sometimes the change went the other way, so *knowed* became *knew*, but usually *-ed* was used. There are still about 250 'irregular' past tense verbs in English, but this is only about half the number that there were in Old English.

In Old English there were two main tenses: past and

present. In Middle English other tenses developed which used *be*, *have*, *shall*, and *will*. *Shall* and *will* began to be used to express the future. *Have* and *be* were both used for the perfect tenses at first, but in the end *have* was used for perfect tenses (as in *they have gone*) and *be* was used for the passive (as in *it was done*). *Be* was also used for the continuous tenses (as in *he is coming*). These tenses were not used very often at this time, but later they were used much more.

When the different noun endings disappeared, people had to put words in a particular order to express meaning. The most common order they used was subject – verb – object. They also used prepositions, for example *in*, *with*, and *by*, instead of noun endings, so the expression **dæges and nihtes** became *by day and by night* in Middle English.

All these grammatical changes were possible because from 1066 until the end of the twelfth century very little was written in English. The official papers of the government and the Church were written in Latin or French. This meant that people were free to make changes to their spoken language very easily.

If English grammar was much simpler by the end of the fifteenth century, its vocabulary was much richer. Between 1100 and 1500, about ten thousand French words were taken into English, three-quarters of which are still in use. French words came into every part of life. The words *blanket*, *ceiling*, *chair*, *dinner*, *fruit*, *lamp*, and *table* described things in the home. Science and the arts were enriched by the ideas and words *dance*, *grammar*, *literature*, *medicine*, *music*, *painting*, *poet*, *square*, and many more. New words arrived to describe the law: *crime*, *judge*, *prison*, and *punish*, for example. And some things in nature received new names: *flower*, *forest*, *mountain*, *river*, and *ocean*.

French (F) words very often replaced Old English (OE) words: for example *people* (from the French **peuple**) replaced **lēode** (OE). But sometimes both the French and the Old English words survived, with small differences in meanings: for example *ask* (OE) and *demand* (F), *wedding* (OE) and *marriage* (F), *king* (OE) and *sovereign* (F). Sometimes French words were used for life in the upper classes, and Old English ones for life in the lower classes. For example, the words for the animals in the fields were Old English (*cows*, *sheep*, and *pigs*) but the words for the meat on the table were French (*beef*, *mutton*, and *pork*).

New English words were made from some of the new

The upper classes at dinner

French words almost immediately. For example, the English *-ly* and *-ful* endings were added to French words to make *gently*, *beautiful*, and *peaceful*.

At the same time several thousand words also entered English from Latin. They came from books about law, medicine, science, literature, or Christianity. These books often used words which could not be translated into English. One translator wrote:

> **. . . there ys many words in Latyn that we have not propre English accordynge thereto.**
>
> *. . . there are many Latin words that we do not have English words for.*

So translators often took the Latin word and made it into an English one. Some words which came into Middle English from Latin at this time were: *admit*, *history*, *impossible*, *necessary*, and *picture*. One important source of Latin words was the first translation of the Bible from Latin to English which was made by John Wycliffe and his followers between 1380 and 1384. They followed the Latin very closely, using many Latin words. More than a thousand Latin words appear for the first time in English in their translation of the Bible.

The changes to the grammar and vocabulary of Middle English did not happen at the same time everywhere. The Old English dialects continued to develop differently from each other. The main dialects in Middle English were similar to those of Old English, but they used different words, word endings, and pronunciations. Understanding people from different places, even those which were quite close, was difficult. There is a famous description by William Caxton, who later brought the printing machine to England, of a conversation in Kent between a farmer's wife and some sailors from London (about eighty kilometres away). The sailors asked for some **eggys** but she did not know this word (in her dialect *eggs* were **eyren**). Thinking that they must be speaking a foreign language, she told them she '**coude speke no frenshe**' (*couldn't speak French*)!

When people wrote, they used the words and pronunciations of their dialects. For example, the sound /x/ in the middle of words was spelt *gh* in the south and *ch* in the north, so *night* (pronounced /nɪxt/ at that time) could be spelt as *night* or *nicht*. One word could have a number of different spellings. There were more than twenty ways of spelling *people* (for example, **pepylle, puple, peeple**), more than five hundred ways of spelling *through*, more than sixty ways of spelling *she* and many more variations. Sometimes a spelling from one dialect has survived, together with the pronunciation from another. For example, *busy* is the spelling from one dialect, but the pronunciation /bɪzi/ is from another.

During this time there were changes to the ways sounds were spelt. The Old English letter ȝ was replaced by *g*, and æ by *a*. *Th* began to be used instead of þ and ð. The Normans introduced *j* and *z*, used *k* more often, and used *u* and *v* for both /ʊ/ and /v/. They replaced *h* with *gh* (*light*), *cw* with *qu* (*queen*), and *sc* with *sh* (*ship*). They used *ch* instead of *c* (*church*) and *ou* instead of *u* (*house*). And in many words they replaced the *u* with an *o* (*love, son*). This was because the letters *m*, *n*, *v*, and *u* were all written in a similar way, making words with groups of these letters difficult to read.

From the thirteenth century, English was used more and more in official papers, and also in literature. Much more literature has survived from this time than from the earlier time of Old English. There are songs, long poems, and explanations of Christianity and the Bible. Here is part of a song from around 1225. It is about the cuckoo – a bird that visits Britain in the early summer.

> **Svmer is icumen in**
> **Lhude sing cuccu!**
> **Groweþ sed and bloweþ med**
> **And springþ þe wde nu.**
> **Sing cuccu!**
> > *Summer has come in,*
> > *Loudly sing, cuckoo!*
> > *The seed grows and the field comes into flower*
> > *And the wood comes up now.*
> > *Sing, cuckoo!*

The greatest writer in Middle English was Geoffrey Chaucer (1343–1400). Chaucer, who lived in London, was both a poet and an important government official. He wrote in the East Midlands dialect (spoken by people living in the Oxford–London–Cambridge triangle) and used many words from French. He also used rhyme, which was used in French and Italian poetry. His best-known work, *The Canterbury Tales*, written in the 1390s, begins with these famous words:

> **Whan that Aprill, with his shoures soote,**
> **The droghte of March hath perced to the roote**
> **And bathed every veyne in swich licuor,**
> **Of which vertu engendred is the flour . . .**
> **Thanne longen folk to goon on pilgrimages . . .**
> > *When April with its sweet showers*
> > *Has pierced the drought of March to the root*
> > *And bathed every vein in such liquid*
> > *From which strength the flower is engendered . . .*
> > *Then people long to go on pilgrimages . . .*

The poem is about a group of ordinary people who journey to the large church at Canterbury together, telling each other stories on the way. They are a varied group of characters, and Chaucer describes them colourfully. There is the Wife (woman) of Bath, the Cook, the Clerk (a student at Oxford), the Man of Law, the Shipman, the Monk, and many others. In their stories and conversations, Chaucer gives us plenty of details about their lives. For example, he makes fun of the French spoken in England:

> **And Frensh she spak ful faire and fetisly,**
> **After the scole of Stratford atte Bowe**
> **For Frensh of Paris was to hir unknowe.**
>
> *And French she spoke extremely beautifully*
> *With an accent from Stratford-at-Bow*
> *Because the French of Paris was unknown to her.*

Chaucer was very good at describing people and also at writing conversation which sounded very real. He had a great effect on writers in the fifteenth century, and many of them copied him.

Another very popular poem in the fourteenth, fifteenth, and sixteenth centuries was *Piers Plowman* by William Langland (1330–1400). In this, Langland wrote about the difficulties of the poor in England, the bad customs of the Church, and also the perfect Christian life. It was a 'dream' poem, in which the writer describes what he has seen in a dream. This kind of poem was popular in France and Italy at the time, but Langland wrote it in the way Old English poems were written. He did not use rhyme; instead in each line he used several words that begin with the same sound. This short piece from near the beginning of the poem shows how he did this:

I was wery, forwandred, and went me to reste
Vnder a brode banke bi a bornes side,
And as I lay and lened and loked in þe wateres,
I slombred in a slepyng, it sweyued so merye.
Thanne gan I meten a merueilouse sweuene –
That I was in a wildernesse, wist I neuer where.

I was tired of wandering and went to rest
Under a broad bank by the side of a brook,
And as I lay and leaned over and looked into the
water,
I fell into a sleep, it sounded so pleasant.
Then I began to dream a marvellous dream –
That I was in a wilderness, I did not know where.

All poems were written to be read out to other people, so the sounds of the words were very important.

A different kind of development in the fourteenth century was the growing use of family names. People began to need these as they moved away from their village or as their village grew larger. Sometimes the family name had the father's name (*Johnson*), as in Anglo-Saxon times. Other names showed where a person lived (*Rivers*, *Hill*), or his town (*Burton*, *Milton*), his country (*French*, *Holland*), or his work (*Cook*, *Fisher*). A person's family name could change five or six times during his lifetime.

In the fifteenth century a machine was brought to England which had a great effect on English. This was the printing machine, which William Caxton brought to London in 1476. Suddenly it was possible to produce thousands of copies of books. But what words and spellings should be used? Caxton wrote:

And that comyn englysshe that is spoken in one shyre varyeth from a nother . . . Certaynly it is harde to playse every man by cause of . . . chaunge of langage.

And the common English that is spoken in one region varies from another . . . Certainly it is hard to please every man because of . . . the change in the language.

Caxton and other printers decided to use the East Midlands dialect, mainly because it was spoken in London and used by government officials. The printers did not make their decisions in a particularly organized way, but slowly standard spellings developed. However, after this time, the sounds in many words changed or disappeared. As a result, there are now thousands of words that are spelt in the way that they were pronounced in Caxton's time. For example, the letter *k* in *knee,* the letter *w* in *wrong*, and the letter *l* in *would* were pronounced at this time.

By the end of the fifteenth century English was starting to be read by thousands of people. In the next century it was read by many more, and used by the great star of English literature – William Shakespeare.

A printing press

6 Modern English begins

The sixteenth century was a time of changes in Europe. Europeans began to explore the Americas, Asia, and Africa, and learning in all areas flowered. In England, the English language grew in order to express a large number of new ideas.

The explorer, Sir Francis Drake

At the beginning of the sixteenth century Latin was the language of learning in all of Europe, and it was seen as richer than English and the other spoken European languages. However, with the growth of education, the introduction of printing, and the new interest in learning, this began to change. More and more people wanted to read books by Roman and Greek writers, and in England they wanted to read them in English. So these books were translated, and other books about learning were written in English. Using English meant that a writer could reach more people, as one sixteenth-century printer explained to a writer who preferred Latin:

Though, sir, your book be wise and full of learning, yet . . . it will not be so saleable.

However, the acceptance of English as a language of learning was not complete until the end of the seventeenth century. For example, in 1687 Isaac Newton chose Latin when he wrote his *Principia,* but fifteen years later he wrote *Opticks* in English.

During the sixteenth and seventeenth centuries, writers in English borrowed about 30,000 words from about fifty languages, mainly to describe new things and ideas. About half of these words are still used today. This very large growth of vocabulary was the main change in English at this time. The new words came mainly from Latin; for example, *desperate, expensive, explain, fact.* Other important sources for new words were French, Italian, Greek, Spanish, and Portuguese. And as the Europeans travelled to more and more places, so words came into English from America, Africa, and Asia. For example *chocolate* and *tomato* came from Mexico; *banana* from Africa, *coffee* from Turkey, and *caravan* from Persia.

Not everyone liked this borrowing of words. Some thought that the strange words were unnecessary and hard to understand. English could express everything quite well without them and the writers were only showing how much Latin they knew. One man, Sir John Cheke, wrote in 1557:

I am of this opinion that our own tung shold be written cleane . . . unmixt . . . with borowing of other tunges.
I think we should write our own language without borrowing words from other languages.

But the borrowing continued, and the new words which survived slowly lost their strangeness.

New words were also added to English in other ways. People were adventurous with language: they used verbs

A Shakespeare play

as nouns (*laugh* and *invite*), or nouns as verbs, or made adjectives from nouns (*shady* from *shade*). Or they put two words together (*chairman*), or they added new parts to words; *un-* to *comfortable*, for example.

The age of Queen Elizabeth the First (Queen of England 1558–1603) was one of a great flowering of literature. There were the poets Spenser and Sidney, and the writers of plays Marlowe, Jonson, and, of course, William Shakespeare.

Shakespeare (1564–1616) is considered the greatest writer of plays. He expressed his understanding of human nature in extraordinarily rich language in his plays and poems. He had the largest vocabulary of any English writer and made about two thousand new words, and a large number of expressions which are now part of Modern English. For example, he wrote: *it's early days* (*it's too soon to know what will happen*); *tongue-tied* (*unable to speak because you are shy*); *the long and the short of it* (*all that needs to be said about something*); *love is blind*. His success and fame during his lifetime meant that his plays had a very great effect on English.

When Elizabeth the First died in 1603 she left no children, so her cousin, King James the Sixth of Scotland, became King James the First of England. In 1604 the new king ordered a translation of the Bible into English. There were many different English translations of the Bible and he wanted to have one main translation. It was made by fifty-four translators who worked together in small groups, using older translations as their guide.

The translators did not follow Shakespeare's example and make new words; instead they used old ones, even ones that were out of date or were becoming unusual. For example, they used *ye* instead of *you* as a subject pronoun, and the *-eth* ending for verbs instead of *-s*. They did not use as many different words as Shakespeare either: he had used twenty thousand and they only used eight thousand. They aimed to make the language sound like poetry when it was read out and usually they succeeded. Here is a short piece from a teaching of Jesus as an example:

Ye have heard that it hath been said, Thou shalt love thy neighbour, and hate thine enemy. But I say unto you, Love your enemies, bless them that curse you, do good to them that hate you . . . That ye may be the children of your Father which is in heaven: for he maketh the sun to rise on the evil and on the good, and sendeth rain on the just and on the unjust.

The King James Bible appeared in 1611 and was read in churches everywhere in England, Scotland, and Wales for the next three hundred years. It was also read in people's homes and taught at school, and for many people it was the only

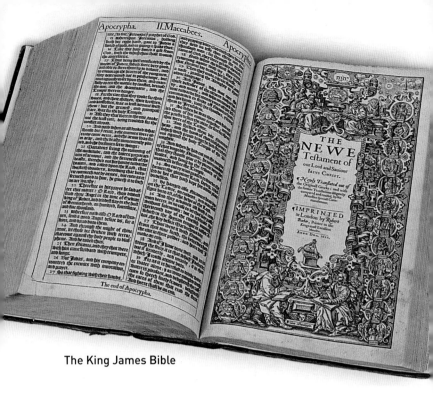

The King James Bible

book that they read again and again. As a result, it had an important effect on the English language. Many expressions from it became part of the language; for example, *the apple of somebody's eye* (*a person who is loved very much by somebody*); *by the skin of your teeth* (*you only just manage to do something*); *the salt of the earth* (*a very honest person*); *the straight and narrow* (*an honest way of living*). Its poetry had a great effect on many English writers in the centuries that followed.

During the sixteenth and seventeenth centuries there were some grammatical changes to English, although not as many as those that had happened to Middle English. People began to use *do* with a main verb. For example, you could say *I know not* or *I do not know*. You could say *I know* or *I do know*. And you could say *know you?* or *do you know?* In the seventeenth century, people began to use *I know*, *I do not know*, and *do you know?* more often. Another verb change was the ending of the third person singular in the present tense. By 1700 the *-th* was no longer used and all verbs took *-s*; for example *loveth* was now *loves*.

Pronouns also changed a little. In 1500 the words *ye* and *you* were used in the same way as *he* and *him*, but by 1700 *ye* had disappeared. *Thou* and *thee* were also used instead of *you* to children or people who were less important than yourself, but these also disappeared in many dialects in the seventeenth century.

Also during this time, the word *its* replaced *his* to talk about things without gender. The leg of a chair was now *its leg* not *his leg*.

Changes in pronunciation were continually taking place. From the middle of the fifteenth century the seven long vowels began to change. For example, in Chaucer's time the word for *life* was pronounced /liːf/ and this became /leɪf/ and then /laɪf/ by the eighteenth century. Similar changes happened to *house*, which was /huːs/ in Chaucer's time. After two changes, it finally arrived at its modern pronunciation /haʊs/.

Sounds in some other words disappeared; for example the /k/ and the /w/ at the beginning of *knee* and *write* were lost. The pronunciation of /t/ in *castle* and the /l/ in *would* also disappeared.

The big growth in vocabulary and the flowering of literature happened when England was quite peaceful. However, in the middle of the seventeenth century this peace was destroyed, and the changes that followed had some interesting effects on the language.

7 Bringing order to English

Charles the First, the son of James the First, was not a popular king, and in 1642 war began between those who wanted him to be king and those who did not. In 1649 he was killed, and England, Wales, and Scotland remained without a king until 1660, when his son Charles the Second returned to England. Charles the Second died in 1685 and his brother James became king in 1685. But James the Second was so unpopular that in 1688 he left England and was replaced by his daughter Mary and her husband William of Orange.

The death of Charles the First

All these changes made people wish for order and regularity in their lives, and some people also wanted more regularity in their language. The great growth in new words between 1530 and 1660 – the fastest in the history of the language – had left people uncertain. What was happening to the language? If so many foreign and newly-made words continued to come into it, would it remain English?

Some people in England wanted to create an official organization to control the English language, similar to the Accademia della Crusca which had been started in Italy in 1582, and the Académie Française which had been started in France in 1635. One of these people was the writer Jonathan Swift, who in 1712 wrote 'A Proposal for Correcting, Improving, and Ascertaining the English Tongue' (*ascertain* here means *fix*). Swift disliked spelling changes, newly fashionable words, the habit of shortening words, and 'bad' grammar. He wanted a group of people to 'fix' the language by making grammar rules, making lists of words that were incorrect, and deciding on correct spellings.

The idea never succeeded, partly because other people realized that change in a language was unavoidable. But it made people think about the need for everyone to use the same spelling and grammar. As a result, different spelling guides, dictionaries, and grammar books began to appear.

Although printing had brought some regularity into spelling, many variations had remained in the sixteenth century, even for personal names. For example, there are six known examples of Shakespeare's name that he wrote himself, and in each one he spelt his name differently. People used their own spellings, which usually showed their own pronunciation. Other variations were introduced to show that words came from Latin. For example, the letter *o* was put into *people*, the letter *b* into *doubt*, and the letter *c* into *scissors*, because the Latin words *populus*, *dubitare*, and *cisorium* had these letters. And different spellings were given to words like *sonne* (a male child) and *sunne* (the star that gives light) which sounded the same but had different meanings. In the end, this freedom to change spellings led to confusion.

In the seventeenth century, people wanted to end this confusion, and the appearance of the first English dictionaries slowly brought about more regularity in spelling. During the eighteenth century, ways of spelling that differed from these dictionaries were seen as incorrect and a sign of stupidity or a bad education. Even today, many people do not like making spelling mistakes, and often use the spell-check tool on their computers.

Dictionaries were not unknown before the seventeenth century, but they were Latin–English ones. The first English–English dictionary appeared in 1604 and was written by a schoolteacher called Robert Cawdrey. It was called *A Table Alphabeticall* and was a list of about 2,500 'hard vsuall English wordes' with explanations of their meaning and sometimes which language they had come from – French (fr) or Greek (gr). Here are some examples of the words in the *Table*:

> (*fr*) *accomplish*, finish, or make an end of;
> *barbarian*, a rude person;
> *eclipse (gr)*, a failing of the light of the sunne or
>   moone;
> *obsolete*, olde, past date, growne out of vse or
>   custome;

A Table Alphabeticall became very popular and similar

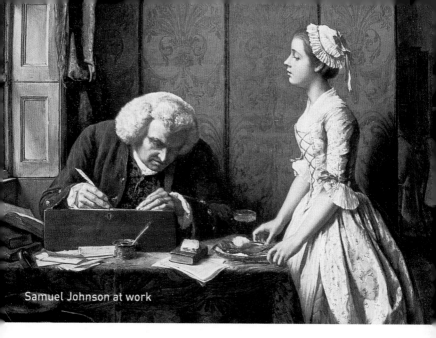

Samuel Johnson at work

dictionaries followed. In the eighteenth century dictionary writers began explaining more ordinary words, not just difficult ones.

In 1746 a group of booksellers asked a young writer called Samuel Johnson to prepare an English dictionary. Johnson worked on this dictionary for nine years, with the help of six other people. For three years he read the works of hundreds of English writers and found examples for words in the dictionary. Then he began to write the meanings of the words. He chose 'hard' words but also many ordinary ones.

When Johnson's *A Dictionary of the English Language* appeared in 1755 it was an immediate success. It explained more than 42,000 words, and as well as the meaning of each word, it gave the pronunciation and history of the word, and sometimes how it was used. A 'cant' word was used only by one group; a 'low' word was informal and not suitable for writing. Johnson gave as many different meanings of a word as he could (there are 66 for *take*). He very often gave an example from literature to show how the word was used. In fact, there are about 114,000 examples in the dictionary, and they are a very large part of it. Most of them come from literature written between 1560 and 1660.

Here are some examples of words and their meanings from Johnson's *Dictionary*:

to búbble To cheat: a cant word.

to nab [*nappa*, Swedish.] To catch unexpectedly; to seize without warning. A word seldom used but in low language.

wóman [*wifman*, *wimman*, Saxon; whence we yet pronounce women in the plural, *wimmen*.] The female of the human race.
That man who hath a tongue is no man,
If with his tongue he cannot win a woman.
Shakespeare.

yéllowboy A gold coin. A very low word.

To *búbble* and *yéllowboy* have both disappeared from English, but *to nab* has survived, with this meaning. It is still an informal word.

The dictionary was not perfect: some of Johnson's explanations were harder to understand than the words themselves, some expressed his personal opinions, and some words were not listed because he disliked them. Also he could not fit in all his examples, so words at the end of the dictionary have fewer examples than those at the beginning. However, it remained the most important English dictionary in Britain for more than a century.

Help with spelling came from dictionaries; help with grammar came from 'grammars'. There had been a few grammar books in the sixteenth and seventeenth centuries, but in the second half of the eighteenth century a very large number suddenly appeared. Many of them told the reader how to write and speak 'correctly', which really meant how to use language in the same way as in serious pieces of literature. They were written for the rich, and aimed to show the difference between the upper and lower classes. They were widely used because people wanted to show that they were educated.

The writers of these grammar books considered that the grammar of much spoken language and of regional dialects (especially Scots) was wrong. They believed that the grammar of English should be the same as that of Latin. For example, they thought that a sentence should not end with a preposition because this did not happen in Latin. So it would be correct to say *I like the town in which I live*, but not *I like the town which I live in*.

The two most widely used grammar books were Robert Lowth's *Short Introduction to English Grammar* which appeared in 1762, and Lindley Murray's *English Grammar* of 1795. These books had a great effect on people's views of grammar in the nineteenth and twentieth centuries and still have some effect today. Some people believe that there is only one 'correct' way of saying things, and argue, for example, about whether it is correct to say *different to* or *different from*. As a result, many first-language speakers of English think that the way they speak and write is incorrect and are ashamed of it. The opposite view – that all ways of expressing an idea are grammatically correct if they can be understood clearly, and that grammar is always changing – is becoming more popular. As a result, some grammar books today simply describe how English is used, instead of telling us how we should speak or write.

There were also some attempts in the second half of the eighteenth century to decide on one correct pronunciation. There were many different ways of pronouncing words, as there were a large number of regional accents. Until this time regional accents were not considered to be bad in any way, or to be a disadvantage. However, many people now wanted to speak correctly as well as write correctly. The first person to teach people 'correct' English pronunciation was an Irishman called Thomas Sheridan. In the 1750s and 1760s he gave talks to large numbers of important people about the 'correct' sounds and pronunciation of English words. Like correct spelling and grammar, correct pronunciation was a sign of education and class. Sheridan wrote in one of his talks:

Pronunciation . . . is a sort of proof that a person has kept good company . . .

Sheridan was followed by John Walker who wrote *A Critical Pronouncing Dictionary and Expositor of the English Language* in 1791. He took the pronunciation of educated people in London as his guide and saw other regional pronunciations as wrong. His dictionary was very successful in both Britain and the US in the nineteenth century. Many people began to feel disadvantaged because they did not speak correctly. It was a long time before regional accents became acceptable again.

8 Modern English grows

If speakers of English from 1800 were able to speak to those of today, they would notice a few differences in grammar and pronunciation, but not very many. For the nineteenth-century speakers the biggest problem would be the extremely large number of new words they would meet.

The developments in science in the last two hundred years have led to hundreds of thousands of new words and expressions for new ideas, machines, materials, plants, animals, stars, diseases, and medicines. Many of these words and expressions are used only by scientists, but others have become part of ordinary English. We know that if we have *bronchitis* (this word first appeared in writing in 1814) we can take *antibiotics* (1944) and we know that our *genes* (1911) come to us from our parents in our *DNA* (1944). We argue about whether we should use *pesticides* (1934) in farming, or *nuclear energy* (1945) to make electricity.

The use of English in different parts of the world and easier and faster communication have together resulted in the appearance of thousands of other new words. Most of them – about 65 per cent – have been made by putting two old words together, for example: *fingerprint* (1859), *airport* (1919), and *street-wise* (1965). The world of computers has introduced many of this type: *online* (1950), *user-friendly* (1977) and *download* (1980). Some new words have been made from Latin and Greek; for example, *photograph* (1839), *helicopter* (1872), *aeroplane* (1874) and *video* (1958). Others are old words that have been given new meanings.

For example, *pilot* (1907) was first used to mean the person who directs the path of ships, and *cassette* (1960) used to mean a small box. About 5 per cent of new words have come from foreign languages, like *disco* (1964) from French, and *pizza* (1935) from Italian. And a few words have come from the names of things we buy or use: for example, *to google* (1999) from *Google*™, the popular Internet search engine, and *podcast* (2004). This word, meaning a recording that you can get from the Internet and play on your computer, comes from *iPod*®, the popular music player, and *broadcast*.

Beginnings or endings have been added to make new words: *disinformation* (1955) is false information; *touchy-feely* (1972) describes people who express their feelings too openly. Sometimes both a beginning and an ending have been added: for example, *unputdownable* (1947) describes a book which is so interesting that you cannot stop reading it. Some words have been shortened: *photo* (1860) for *photograph*, *plane* (1908) for *aeroplane*, and *TV* (1948) for *television*. Some words have put together sounds from two other words: for example *motel* (1925), a hotel for car drivers, is made from *motor* and *hotel*. Only a very few new words have not been made from other words. Two examples are *nylon* (1938) to describe a man-made material, and *flip-flop* (1970), a type of shoe that makes a noise as you walk.

The growth in vocabulary is clear when we look at the making of the *Oxford English Dictionary* (*OED*) in the nineteenth and twentieth centuries. This dictionary contains all English words since 1150, even those that are no longer used. It shows, with examples, when each word was first used in writing and how the meaning of a word has changed over the centuries.

Finding all this information was a very big job, although

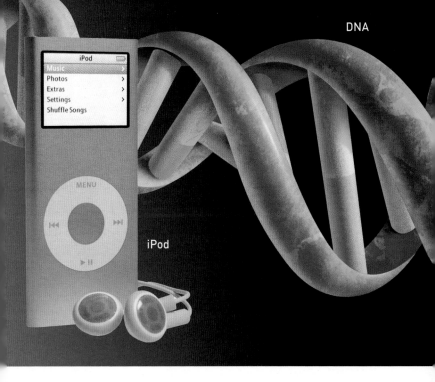

DNA

iPod

no one realized at the beginning exactly *how* big. A Scotsman called James Murray was appointed as the director of work on the dictionary in 1879, and the plan was to finish the job in ten years. Murray organized a very large reading programme: hundreds of people sent him examples of how words were used. After five years, the first part of the dictionary was completed, but it only went from A to ANT. Everyone realized that the job was going to take a lot longer than ten years; in fact, it took another forty-four. Sadly, Murray did not live to see its completion: he died in 1915, aged seventy-eight, while he was working on the letter U. However, he knew that he had helped to make a dictionary which would give a detailed history of the English language.

The first *OED* was completed in 1928 and explained the meaning and history of 414,800 words and expressions, with examples from literature and other writing. The second *OED*, completed in 1989, explained the meanings of 615,100 words,

James Murray and
the first *OED*

although many of these – perhaps 20 per cent – are no longer used. It shows how the words were or are used and has 2.5 million examples from all kinds of books. It contains some scientific words and words from North America, Australia, New Zealand, South Africa, the Caribbean, India, and Pakistan, but not all scientific or regional words in English.

The second *OED* went online in 2000, and every three months new material is added to this online dictionary, as part of the writing of the third *OED*. At the same time work is continuing on the words and meanings already in the dictionary, and changes are made if necessary. For some words there are more details of their history to add, or earlier or later examples. North American and other regional pronunciations are given as well as British ones. These are the first changes to Murray's work since the first *OED* appeared in 1928. The work on the third *OED*, begun in 1993, will probably finish in 2018.

The *OED* has had a great effect on our knowledge and understanding of English. It has given us a lot of information about the history of words and expressions and has helped us understand how language changes over time.

The way dictionaries are made has been changed by computers. There are now extremely large collections of examples of English works on computer that dictionary writers can use. They can look through these for examples of words and see how they are used, and they can use the Internet to search for words. They can also ask readers all over the world to send examples to a website, which means that they can get words from a very wide variety of places. Information about informal words and slang, for example, is now much easier to find because of the Internet. And when a dictionary is written, it can be kept on computer and put on a website.

For about the past hundred years new words have been able to travel fast around the English-speaking world because of the telephone, newspapers, radio, television, films, pop music, and the Internet. These ways of communication can reach extremely large numbers of people. Television and radio have also influenced pronunciation.

In the 1920s the British Broadcasting Corporation (BBC) chose an accent for all its speakers to use on the radio. This was the accent of the educated: people in government, at the universities, in the army, and the Church. It was known as 'Received Pronunciation' or 'RP', or 'the King's English'. The use of RP on radio and later on television meant that more people heard it and thought that it was the accent that socially important people used. It was not acceptable to use strong regional accents on television and radio, or in teaching and government. However, in the 1960s social differences in Britain began to break down, and regional accents became more acceptable everywhere. And as the number of radio and television programmes grew, more people with different accents had to be employed. Today RP is no longer an important accent and most educated people in England (not Scotland, Wales, or Northern Ireland) now speak a kind of RP which has some of their regional accent in it. Television has also made some regional dialects popular. For example, you can now hear parts of the dialect called Estuary English, which is from London and the south-east of England, in many other parts of England. (See Chapter 10 for more about dialects.)

The biggest technological development in recent years is, of course, the Internet. People can now communicate in writing on their websites, through e-mail, on message boards, and in chat rooms. The Internet has had a number of effects on English. Firstly, new words have been made to describe the Internet itself and its activities; for example, *cyberspace* (1982), *e-mail* (1982), *website* (1993), and *blog* (1999). Or new meanings have been given to old words; for example, *link* (1951), *chat* (1985), *virtual* (1987), and *surf* (1992).

Secondly, people have developed a new informal way of writing in chat rooms and on message boards. Many users shorten a lot of words, using just single letters or numbers, and often they do not use capital letters or much punctuation. Many use their own spellings, or spellings that are often used in chat rooms. Some people also use smileys (little pictures of faces with different expressions) to show how they feel. They also use groups of letters for some expressions. For example: *lol* means *laughing out loud*; *btw* means *by the way*; *bbl* means *be back later*. Sentences you could see in a chat room or on a message board are:

r u alryt? (*Are you all right?*)

im good thx ☺ (*I'm good, thanks*)

duz ne1 know how 2 make carrot cake? (*Does anyone know how to make carrot cake?*)

People also use similar language when they send messages by phone. For example:

thx 4 ur msg. How r u? (*Thanks for your message. How are you?*)

im fine. c u @ work (*I'm fine. See you at work.*)

After learning the rules of written English at school, many people are now enjoying playing with language: breaking the old rules and making new ones.

Sending text messages

9 English in the US

'England and America are two countries separated by the same language,' wrote George Bernard Shaw in 1942. Is this true today? Do Americans speak a different kind of English from the British? If so, why? And why do they speak English at all?

To answer the last question we must go back to the year 1607, when a group of English people sailed across the Atlantic and reached the east coast of America. They called their settlement Jamestown, after King James the First and they called that part of the country Virginia. They were not the first English people in America: in 1585 and 1587 people had tried to settle on the island of Roanoke, in what is now North Carolina. They were not the first Europeans to settle in America either: the Spanish had lived in Florida since 1565. But the people of Jamestown were the first successful English settlers, and they were followed by other English adventurers who also settled in Virginia.

Then in 1620 more English settlers landed north of Virginia, in what became Massachusetts, New England. These were the people from the ship called the *Mayflower*, who came because they wanted to follow a different kind of Christianity from the kind in England. Others followed, and by 1640 about 25,000 English people were living in New England.

At this time, sailors from England and other European countries were taking Africans to America and selling them as slaves. The first twenty African slaves were brought to America in 1619. The Africans had to live in terrible conditions during the long sea voyage, and many did not survive. This inhuman business was ended in 1808, but people were allowed to own slaves until the end of the American Civil War in 1865. By that time there were more than 4 million Africans living in America.

During the seventeenth and eighteenth centuries more and more people arrived in America. The British government sent prisoners to America as a punishment, and other settlers arrived from France, Germany, the Caribbean, and the north of Ireland. The people from the north of Ireland were called the Scots-Irish (because their families had moved to Ireland from Scotland). By the year of American independence (1776), about one in seven settlers in America was Scots-Irish.

In the nineteenth century, large numbers of people left Ireland, Germany, Italy, and other European countries for

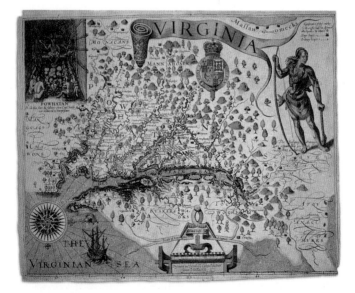

A map of Virginia, 1612

America. Many were Jews from Central and Eastern Europe. By 1900 there were 75 million people living in America. In the later part of the twentieth century people from Asia and Spanish-speaking countries also arrived, and by 2000 there were more than 280 million people in America.

American English developed from the languages used by these different people. The first English settlers immediately discovered animals, birds, and plants that were new to them, and which needed names in English. Sometimes the settlers used English words (for example *blackbird* for a bird that looked similar to the English blackbird). Sometimes they made new words from other English words, for example *backwoods* (*a forest with few people*), and *bluegrass* (*a kind of grass with blue-green leaves*). They also named thousands of places and rivers using words from the languages of the Native Americans; for example, Massachusetts, Mississippi, Potomac. The Spanish and French controlled some parts of the country until the nineteenth century, so some place names are from French (like Detroit, St Louis, and Illinois) and some from Spanish (like Los Angeles, San Francisco, and Santa Fe). New York was first New Amsterdam, until the English

Arriving in America:　　Dutch explorers　　African slaves
English settlers

took it in 1664, and the names Brooklyn (from **Breukelyn**), Harlem (**Haarlem**), and the Bronx (**Bronck's**) are reminders of its Dutch beginnings. Occasionally the English settlers borrowed words for things or people from other European languages, for example, *cookie* from Dutch, *cent* and *dime* from French, *plaza* from Spanish. The settlers also began to give some old words new meanings: for example *bill* began to mean *a piece of paper money*, and it replaced *note*.

Some words from the English of the seventeenth century survive in American English but are not used now in British English. For example, *fall* meaning *autumn*, *mad* meaning *angry*, and *gotten* as the past participle of 'get' (as in *Your dinner has gotten cold*).

Some of the pronunciation of the first settlers also survives in Modern American English. They pronounced the *a* in *grass* /æ/ as in *hat*, because the long /ɑː/ sound only began to be used instead of /æ/ in England in the eighteenth century. This short /æ/ is part of American pronunciation today. Most Americans also pronounce the *r* at the end of words (for example *car*) and before a consonant (for example *hard*) as the early settlers did.

German immigrants   Italian immigrants   Jewish immigrants

As the settlers moved west in the nineteenth century, they added many colourful new expressions to American English. These are now part of British English too; for example, *to face the music* (*to accept the unpleasant results of your actions*); *to kick the bucket* (*to die*); *hot under the collar* (*angry*). Some expressions come from the time when the railroads were built: *to go off the rails* (*to behave strangely*), and *to reach the end of the line* (*to be unable to do any more with something*).

American English has borrowed only a few words from the languages spoken by the nineteenth-century immigrants. The reason for this is social. People who had recently arrived in the US wanted to become American, and they and their children learned English to do so. However, some words and expressions from other languages *have* found their way into American English. For example, *check* (*a bill for food or drinks*), and *kindergarten* (*a place where very young children play and learn*) have come from German; *pasta*, *spaghetti*, and other words for food have come from Italian; from Yiddish, the language of the East European Jews, there

Building a railroad

are *schmuck* (*a stupid person*), and *shlep* (*to pull*, or *a long, tiring journey*).

African-Americans developed their own varieties of English which are all known today as African-American English or Black English. They had an effect on American English, especially in the twentieth century when large numbers of African-Americans left the South and moved north. Some words that they brought to American English are *jazz* (*a kind of music first developed by African-Americans*), *cool* meaning *excellent*; and *dude*, another word for *man*.

At the time of independence in 1776, Americans began to take an interest in their language. They wanted to be separate from Britain in every way, and to feel proud of their country and way of life. Someone who felt very proud of American English was a teacher called Noah Webster (1758–1843). Between 1783 and 1785 Webster wrote a speller, a grammar, and a reader for American schools. The speller was later sold as *The American Spelling Book*, and was extremely successful, selling more than 80 million copies in the next hundred years. With the money from the speller, Webster was able to write dictionaries. In these, he wanted to show that American English was as good as British English, and that Americans did not have to copy the British. His first dictionary appeared in 1806, followed in 1828 by his famous work *An American Dictionary of the English Language*. This was longer than Johnson's dictionary (it explained about 70,000 words) and so gave American English the same importance as British English in the minds of Americans.

Sixty years earlier, Benjamin Franklin had suggested many changes to English spelling, and his ideas influenced Webster. In both his dictionaries Webster suggested new spellings, and many of these are now the accepted American spellings;

for example, *center*, *color*, and *traveled*. Some of his other suggestions were not followed: *soop* (*soup*), *bred* (*bread*), and *medicin* (*medicine*), for example. Webster also influenced American pronunciation by saying that each part of a word must be clearly pronounced: for example, *se-cre-ta-ry* not *se-cre-try*.

So what are the differences between American and British English today? As well as differences in pronunciation, there are some small differences in grammar and spelling. But the main difference is in vocabulary. Thousands of words are used differently. Firstly, different words are sometimes used in American and British English to talk about the same thing. For example, the street-level floor of a building is called *the first floor* in American English, and *the ground floor* in British English. You drive on the *freeway* in the US, but on the *motorway* in Britain.

There are also different expressions in American and British English. For example, the American expressions *to drop the ball* (*to make a mistake*), *to be in the chips* (*to suddenly have a lot of money*), and *to go south* (*to become less valuable*) are not used in British English. Similarly many British expressions are not part of American English.

Some British people dislike the effect of American English on British English, but this has not stopped thousands of American words entering British English and becoming completely accepted; for example, *OK* (1840), *supermarket* (1933), *teenager* (1941), and *fast food* (1951).

Although there are clear differences between the American and British varieties of English, television, music, films, and more recently the Internet have helped people on both sides of the Atlantic to understand each other's English more easily.

10 All kinds of English

I'm ganen doon the toon the day. (*I'm going into town today.* North-eastern England)

Dinna fash yoursel. (*Don't upset yourself.* Central and Southern Scotland)

They work hard, isn't it? (*They work hard, don't they?* Wales)

I'm after seeing him. (*I've just seen him.* Ireland)

Y'all come here! (*Come here everyone!* Southern US)

It's a beaut! (*It's wonderful!* Australia)

She sing real good. (*She sings very well.* Jamaica)

I am not knowing. (*I don't know.* India)

Make you no min am. (*Take no notice of him/her.* Nigeria)

All over the world, people speaking English as a first or second language use different vocabulary, grammar, and accents in a large number of varieties of English. A variety of English is a type of English spoken by one group of people. In each English-speaking country one variety of English is used nationally. This is the 'Standard English' of that country. It is taught in schools and spoken on radio and television. Everyone in the country uses the same grammar, vocabulary, and spelling when they use their country's Standard English, though they may speak it with different accents. Different countries have different Standard Englishes. For example, Standard Australian English is different from Standard British English.

In England, as well as Standard British English there are regional and social dialects of English. The most noticeable differences between them are those of pronunciation. A well-known difference is the sound of the vowel *a* in words like *grass*. In the south *grass* is pronounced as /grɑːs/, and in the north as /græs/. The vowel *u* in words like *up* is pronounced /ʌp/ in the south and /ʊp/ in the north. In some parts of the north *happy* is pronounced as /hæpɪ/ or /hæpe/, and in the north-east *night* is pronounced as /niːt/.

In Estuary English, which began in the south-east of England, some sounds are pronounced in the same way as in Cockney – the dialect of East London. The /t/ in the middle and at the end of words disappears; so the word *better* becomes /beʔə/ and the word *what* becomes /wɒʔ/. /θ/ becomes

David Beckham uses Estuary English

/f/ and /ð/ becomes /v/, so *think* becomes /fɪŋk/ and *mother* becomes /mʌvə/. This dialect has become popular among young people because of radio and television.

Many new British dialects are developing. People from the Caribbean, India, Pakistan, and Eastern Europe have settled in the big cities in Britain. Young people from these groups use some of their own languages with the local dialect, their friends copy them, and in this way they make a new dialect.

There are also differences in grammar between the dialects. Some of the older dialects from the countryside use grammatical forms which Standard English has lost: for example, *thee* and *thou* for *you* singular. Modern dialects also use grammar that is different from Standard English: *I don't want no dinner* (*I don't want any dinner*), *them books* (*those books*), *she ain't come* (*she hasn't come*). And in some dialects young people use *innit?* at the end of a sentence. For example, *Now I can start calling you that, innit?* (*can't I?*), *We need to go now, innit?* (*don't we?*)

All dialects have some words and expressions, both old and new, that are different from Standard English. For example, *butty* (*a piece of bread and butter*) has been used in the north of England since the nineteenth century; *nang* (*good*) has come in recently to Cockney in London from Bengali.

Outside England, in Scotland, Wales, Northern Ireland, and the Republic of Ireland, there are other varieties of English. Scots is very different from Standard British English – more so than any other British variety. There are many differences in pronunciation, grammar, and vocabulary. Some

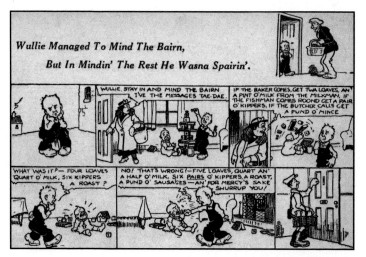

An example of Scots

Scots vocabulary is also used in northern English dialects (for example, *bairn* for *child* and *lass* for *girl*), but a very large number of words (20,000 are listed in one book) are used only in Scots.

The English spoken in Wales also has its own character. The voice rises and falls in a way which is similar to Welsh, and there are some words and expressions which have been borrowed from Welsh. Sometimes word order is changed to give something more importance; for example, *Great those are!* (*Those are great!*)

In Northern Ireland, Scots has had a great effect on English because large numbers of settlers came to Ireland from Scotland in the seventeenth century. For example, *wee* (a Scots word meaning *little*) is used. In the Republic of Ireland, Gaelic and dialects from the west of England have had the most effect on English. Gaelic is still spoken in the west of Ireland and the dialects of English in this part of the country show its effect more strongly than others. For example, people say *Is it cold you are?* (*Are you cold?*) or *He's after doing that* (*He's just done that*). The Irish English spoken on radio and television is closer to Standard British English.

From the seventeenth century onwards, regional varieties of English were taken to North America, the Caribbean, Australia, New Zealand, Africa, and Asia, and they can still be heard in the varieties of English in these places. For example, in some dialects of American English there are many similarities to Irish English in pronunciation and some in grammar. *Youse* which means *you* plural comes from Irish English, and so does *anymore* in positive sentences (for example, *They live here anymore* which is *They live here now* in British English).

The three main regional dialects of American English are Northern, Midland, and Southern. These show the movement of settlers to the West. Settlers from New England in the north-east moved past the Great Lakes; those from the middle of the east coast moved through the middle of the country, and those in the south went along the coast to the south. Because the Midland dialect is spoken over the largest area, and by perhaps two-thirds of the people, this dialect is the best known outside America, and is sometimes called 'General American'.

African-American English, or Black English, was born between the seventeenth and nineteenth centuries, when millions of people from West Africa were brought to America and the Caribbean to work as slaves on large farms growing cotton and sugar. The slave buyers and the African slaves communicated on the slave ships in pidgin English – a simple kind of English that allowed speakers of different languages to communicate with each other. When the Africans arrived in America and the Caribbean they continued to use pidgin English both with the slave owners and with each other, as they often spoke different African languages. Later, this pidgin English developed into a creole language when the slaves' children and grandchildren started to use it as their first language. African-American English probably developed from this creole. Today African-American English has some grammatical differences from American English; for example, *she come* (*she's coming*), *you crazy* (*you're crazy*), *twenty cent* (*twenty cents*).

French, Dutch, Spanish, and Portuguese creoles have also had a big effect on the English of the Caribbean. (Other influences have been local languages and Hindi spoken by settlers from India.) In the Caribbean today there are a large number of English creoles, as well as local varieties of Standard English. Each creole has a different vocabulary, but their grammar and pronunciation are similar. For example, there is *de* for *the*, *ting* for *thing*, and *ax* for *ask*. Here is part of a poem in Jamaican Creole by Louise Bennett. It is called 'Noh Lickle Twang!' ('Not Even a Little Accent!'). In it, the poet complains that her son has come back from America without an American accent:

> **Ef you want please him meck him tink**
> **Yuh bring back someting new.**
> **Yuh always call him 'Pa' dis evenin'**
> **Wen him come sey 'Poo'.**
> > *If you want to please him [your*
> > *father] make him think*
> > *You've brought back something new.*
> > *You always call him 'Pa'; this*
> > *evening*
> > *When he comes say 'Poo'.*

Louise Bennett

The English of Canada is similar to both American and British English. It uses some British words and some American ones. For example, Canadians fill their cars with *gas* (American English) but ask for the *bill* (British English). They often add *eh?* to the end of a sentence. For example, *It's cold, eh?* The pronunciation of Canadian English is very close to that of American English, but one difference is the pronunciation of /aʊ/, which Canadians pronounce as /əʊ/ in some words. So the word *about* sounds like *aboat*.

Australian English has developed from a number of varieties of English. Most of the 130,000 prisoners sent to Australia between 1788 and 1840, and the 'free settlers' who joined them, came from the south and east of England,

Scotland, and Ireland. The vowels in Australian English sound similar to those in Cockney (for example, *today* sounds similar to RP *to die*) and some Australian expressions are from British, Irish, and American English. American words are starting to be used more as a result of American films and television programmes. Some words for plants and animals, and many place names, have come from Aboriginal languages. There are many very colourful expressions in Australian English; for example: *to be as full as a boot* (*to be very drunk*), *first in, best dressed* (*the first people to do something will have an advantage*), *couldn't lie straight in bed* (*to be very dishonest*).

New Zealand English and South African English have some similarities to Australian English in their pronunciation because all three countries were settled by English speakers at about the same time. Each variety has small pronunciation differences, though, and its own vocabulary. In New Zealand English there are words from Māori, and in South African English there are words from Afrikaans and African languages.

Other countries were also governed by the British in the nineteenth and twentieth centuries; for example, India, Singapore, Nigeria, Kenya, Papua New Guinea. Others were governed by the US: the Philippines and Puerto Rico. In many of these countries English is an official language, although it is not most people's first language. In these countries, the local languages and their regional dialects have an effect on the pronunciation, grammar, vocabulary, and use of English, and new varieties of English develop. These are sometimes called 'New Englishes'. They have not been studied very deeply, or for very long, so it is difficult to get a clear picture of each variety. However, people are collecting information about these new varieties and studying them, so in future we will know more about them.

In the newest varieties of English, words from another language are very often used with English ones. These varieties are often given amusing names. For example, in the US some Spanish speakers speak 'Spanglish' which uses English and Spanish words in the same sentence. English words are borrowed and given Spanish sounds and spelling, such as *parquin* (*parking*). Other examples of these varieties are 'Singlish' in Singapore, 'Hinglish' in India (Hindi and English), and 'Taglish' in the Philippines (Tagalog and English).

All these varieties of English, from countries where English is used either as a first language or as a second language, are used more and more by writers and film-makers. In this way, many users of English are able to hear and read more than their own variety and words and expressions can cross from one variety to another.

A sign in 'Spanglish'

11 Jargon and slang

Jargon and slang are kinds of English that are not part of Standard English. Jargon is the difficult or strange language used by a group of people to describe things that the rest of us do not know about. For example, doctors, lawyers, university teachers, and business managers all use words and expressions that the rest of us do not understand.

In business, some of this jargon comes from the world of the Internet. For example, if you are in a big meeting with someone and they suggest discussing something with you *offline,* they mean they want to talk to you privately later. Other management jargon is not from the world of computers. For example, a manager could ask you: 'What could you bring to the table if you got this job? Can you think outside the box?' This means, '*What could you give to our team? Can you think in unusual ways to find answers to problems?'*

There is also a lot of jargon in sports that is only understood by people who do these sports. For example, if you are not a mountain biker, you will probably not know what a *bunny hop* is. (It is a jump that mountain bikers make when they come off the ground with both wheels. *Bunny* is an informal word for *rabbit*, a small animal that jumps a lot.) People use jargon because they need to describe very detailed things or ideas and the rest of us have to try and understand it.

Slang is an extremely informal kind of language – much more informal than jargon. It is usually only spoken; jargon

A bunny hop

is often written as well as spoken. Slang usually belongs to a group of people who use it to show that they belong to that group – and that others do not. Sometimes they need language that others will not understand. For example, young people, people in prison, and people in the army all have their own kinds of slang. Slang is colourful, funny, and often cruel. It gives us new words for things we already have words for (for example, *rock up* for *arrive*). Jargon, on the other hand, often gives us new words for new things or ideas.

Most slang changes quite quickly, because the people who use it need to make new words to keep confusing outsiders. But some slang lasts longer: *pig* for *policeman* has been used since 1800. Other words become part of the informal language. For example, *row*, meaning *noisy argument*, was slang in Britain in the eighteenth century. Some slang words become part of Standard English. For example, *joke*, meaning *something that someone says to make people laugh*, was a slang word at the end of the seventeenth century. Other slang words change their meaning over time. For example, in American English *previous* meant *arriving too soon* in the

1900s; in 1920 it meant *tight* (of clothes) and in the 1970s it meant *a bit rude*.

The slang used by African-American musicians has had a great effect on British slang since the Second World War. This effect has grown recently as American rap music with its fast spoken rhymes has become popular around the world. Words from the US can now reach Britain in weeks through the Internet and television. For example, *awesome*, *wicked*, and *bad* (meaning *excellent*) have been widely used by young people in Britain but they were first used in the US.

Many slang words show that you like or dislike something. For example, in British slang *lush* means *lovely*, *Boom!* means *the very best*, and *minging* means *bad*. In Britain a stupid person is called a *div*, in the US a *dummy*, in Australia a *dill* or a *boofhead*. A pretty but stupid girl is a *bimbo* in Britain and the US, a boring person is a *dweeb* in the US, a lazy man is a *bludger* in Australia. A good-looking person is *spunky* in Australia or *buff* in the US and Britain.

The basic things in life are often given slang words: food is *grub* in Britain and the US (a word that has been used since the seventeenth century) and *tucker* in Australia; money is *wonga* or *dough* in Britain, *green* or *moolah* in the US. There are also many words for having no money, being drunk, being sick, crimes and criminals, the police, and different parts of the body.

Australians are very proud of their slang and often use it. It has many shortened words: for example, *arvo* for *afternoon*, *Aussie* for *Australian*, *brekkie* for *breakfast*, and *sunnies* for *sunglasses*. The Cockneys of East London are also proud of their 'rhyming slang' which is now widely used. In this slang, part of the slang expression rhymes with the word in Standard English. For example: *garden plant* means *aunt*,

Grandmaster Flash – one of the first rap musicians

plates of meat means *feet*, *bread and honey* means *money*. It can become more difficult to understand when the rhyming word is not used. For example, *I need some bread* means *I need some money*. Today most new rhyming slang uses famous names. For example, *Britney Spears* means *beers*. Rhyming slang is also used in Australia and the US.

New slang words are always appearing and disappearing. Some words are used only by the small groups that made them, others become part of national or international slang, and others cross into ordinary spoken language. In this way, slang is an important source of new words in Standard English.

12 The future of English

'It's good that everything's gone, except their language,
which is everything.'
(Derek Walcott, 'North and South', 1982)

'. . . we no longer control English in any meaningful way.
It is no longer our ship, but the sea.'
(Andrew Marr, 1998)

The Jamaican poet Derek Walcott knows that English is still used in countries that were governed by Britain; the British journalist Andrew Marr recognizes that English does not belong just to the British or Americans, but to the whole world. English continues to be used by speakers of other languages all over the world, and to be changed by those languages. But how will this situation change in the future?

In Britain, the US, Canada, Australia, and New Zealand, English will remain the first language of most people, but will continue to change. New slang and dialects will develop, often from groups of people who speak other languages, for example, Spanish in the US and South Asian languages in Britain. In countries where English is used as a second language, it is possible that new languages will develop which use English and local languages. An example of this is Sheng, a new Kenyan language which uses words from English, Swahili, and other African languages.

One guess is that the number of people who can use English well will continue to grow – to over half the people in the world by 2050, some believe – and that English will remain a world language for many years. In this view, the US will remain the richest country in the world, American popular music and films will continue to be fashionable, and English will still be the language of science, communications technology, international business, education at universities, and television news. English will continue to change, but it will not lose its importance in the world.

However, other people think that the future of English as a world language is not so certain. Mandarin Chinese, Spanish, and Arabic may become other world languages, as the numbers of people who speak these languages continue to grow, and the countries where they are spoken become richer. Although international business may grow, some of it may be with countries in the same part of the world, and other shared languages may be used instead of English. There are now more users of the Internet who do not speak English as a first language than those who do, so businesses and organizations have to provide information and services in different languages for these Internet users. In education, international students may go to countries that are nearby: for example, more Asian students may go to China. English may also lose its importance and popularity in the world of films and music.

If English remains a world language, some governments may try to stop its use in their own countries. They may fear that the use of English will endanger their own languages and customs. Some countries have already tried to stop the borrowing of English words by passing laws against the use of foreign words in some situations (for example, France in 1977 and 1994, and Poland in 1997). In other countries, India, for example, there is much discussion about teaching

Learning English in China

children in English in schools. Some consider it harmful for the children's learning, and also for the survival of their own languages. Others, however, think that it is necessary for the country's future survival in the world.

If English *does* remain a world language, how will it change? Will it break up into a number of different languages, as Latin developed into French, Spanish, Portuguese, Romanian, and Italian? Or will the different varieties disappear and only one kind of English survive?

It seems probable that as English is used internationally more and more, the need for a standard grammar and vocabulary, standard spelling rules, and some standard pronunciation will remain. Perhaps a new simpler kind of 'World Standard English' will develop from the regional varieties, one which all users can easily use and understand. If a sound is hard for people to make, and words can be understood without it, then it could disappear. For example *th* is difficult for many speakers, and does not have to be pronounced as /θ/ or /ð/, so this sound could change.

On the other hand, it seems that the number of regional varieties of English is growing and will continue to grow. These varieties may become more and more different from the World Standard kind of English, although they may not become separate languages because they will have a lot of contact with standard kinds of English through television, radio, and the Internet.

As the number of second- and foreign-language speakers of English grows larger than the number of first-language speakers, other languages will have a greater effect on English. Extremely large numbers of words from other languages will probably continue to cross into English at great speed.

The next step in the history of the English language is hard to see clearly because it depends on many things: changes in business, science, technology, and numbers of people. Will the speakers of English at the end of this century speak a very different English from the one we use now? Who will use it, and how? These are interesting questions for all users of English.

GLOSSARY

adjective a word that describes a person or thing e.g. *tall, blue*

article the words *a, an,* and *the*

Bible the holy book of the Christian religion

chat room a place on the Internet where you can communicate with other people

Christianity the religion based on the teachings of Jesus Christ; **Christian** (*n* & *adj*) connected with this religion

class (here) a group of people of the same social level

communicate to exchange information, ideas etc with someone; (*n*) **communication**

conquest the act of taking control of a country by force

consonant any letter of the alphabet except *a, e, i, o,* or *u*

creole a language that is a mixture of a European language and a local language, and that is spoken as a first language

dialect a variety of a language spoken in one area which differs from the standard language in grammar, words, and pronunciation

education a process of learning and teaching to improve knowledge; **educated** (*adj*) having had a high standard of education

express (*v*) to show your feelings or opinions through words

flower (*v*) to develop and become successful

gender (in some languages) a way of putting words into groups – masculine, feminine, and neuter

govern to have legal control of a country; (*n*) **government**

grammar the rules in a language for changing the form of words and joining them together into sentences; (*adj*) **grammatical**

immigrant a person who has come to live permanently in a country that is not their own

industrial connected with the production of goods in factories

influence a person or thing that affects the way things happen or develop

informal (of language) relaxed, not serious or correct

Internet   the international network of computers that lets you see information from all over the world

invade   to enter a country by force in order to take control of it

kingdom   a country controlled by a king or queen

literature   pieces of writing, especially novels, plays, and poems

message board   a place on a website where you can read or write messages

monk   a man who works for the church and who lives with other monks in a special building

noun   a word that refers to a person, place, thing, or quality (e.g. *mother, street, box, hope*)

object   the part of a sentence that shows the person or thing affected by the verb

official (*n* & *adj*)   a person in a position of authority; chosen or agreed by such a person

online   connected to the Internet

ordinary   not unusual or different

organization   a group of people who work together to do something

Parliament   the group of people chosen to make and change the laws of a country

personal pronoun   the words *I, me, you, he, him* etc.

plural   the form of a noun or verb that refers to more than one thing

poem   a piece of writing where words are chosen for their sound and arranged in lines, expressing something imaginatively; **poet** a person who writes poems; **poetry** poems in general

print   to put words onto paper using a machine in order to make books

pronounce   to make the sound of a word or letter in a particular way; (*n*) **pronunciation**

region   one part of a country

replace   to take the place of

rhyme   the use of words that end with the same sound in a poem

science the study of natural things; **scientific** (*adj*) connected with science

settle to make a place in a new country your home

singular the form of a noun or verb that refers to one thing

slave a person who belongs to another person and has to work for them for no money

source a place where something begins or comes from

spread (*v & n*) to be used by more and more people; to move to more and more places

standard (of language) believed to be correct and used by most people

technology the use of scientific knowledge to build and make things; (*adj*) **technological**

tense a verb form that shows the time of something happening, either in the past, present, or future

translate to express the meaning of something in a different language; (*n*) **translation**

verb a word that expresses an action or state (e.g. *walk, be*)

vocabulary all the words in a language

vowel the letters *a, e, i, o,* and *u,* and the sounds that they represent

website a place on the Internet where you can find out information about something

ACTIVITIES

Before Reading

1 **How much do you know about the language of English? Fill in the blanks with these items.**

an, b, e, feminine, from, -ful, full stop, get, i, -ing, masculine, question mark, s, the, turn, with

vowels: _____, _____   articles: _____, _____

consonants: _____, _____   verbs: _____, _____

prepositions: _____, _____   endings: _____, _____

punctuation: _____, _____   genders: _____, _____

2 **How much do you know about the history of the language? Choose the best words to complete these sentences.**

  1 English developed from the languages spoken by invaders from *northern Europe / China*.
  2 The English words for some of the days of the week come from the names of *kings and queens / gods and goddesses*.
  3 A place with a name ending in *-ford* is usually near *a river / a mountain*.
  4 For more than three hundred years after 1066, all the kings of England spoke *German / French*.
  5 Six hundred years ago, the letter *k* in *knee* was *pronounced / not pronounced*.

3 **Can you name some words that have come into your language from English? Who uses them? How do you feel about the arrival of English words in your language? Why do you feel this?**

ACTIVITIES

While Reading

Read Chapter 1, then complete these sentences with the correct words.

communication, international, quarter, settled, simple, spread, traffic, widely

1 English is spoken very _____. About a _____ of all the people in the world use English in some way.

2 'Airspeak' is a _____ form of English used in international air _____ control.

3 English started to _____ around the world about three hundred years ago, when many British people _____ in other countries.

4 In the twentieth century, air travel made more _____ business possible. Telephones and computers also made faster _____ possible.

Read Chapter 2, then put these events in the correct order.

1 The Romans left Britain.

2 Wessex became the strongest kingdom in England.

3 The Kurgan people began to travel across Europe and Asia.

4 Jutes, Angles, and Saxons from northern Europe settled in Britain.

5 Some British people learnt to speak and write Latin.

6 The Celts settled in Britain.

7 The people of England and south-east Scotland organized themselves into seven kingdoms.

8 The Romans invaded Britain.

9 The Celts began to leave their homeland in central Europe.

Read Chapter 3, then rewrite these untrue sentences with the correct information.

1 The name *Dover* comes from the Celtic word for *mountain*.
2 The Anglo-Saxons borrowed the words for *street* and *wall* from the Celts.
3 The word *school* came from German, which was used a lot by monks.
4 *Friday* was named after the Anglo-Saxon goddess of war.
5 King Alfred won an important battle against the Romans.
6 King Alfred decided to make Greek the language of education and literature.
7 Most towns with names ending in *–thorpe* are in the west of England.

Before you read Chapter 4, can you guess the answers to these questions?

1 When William and his army come to fight Harold's army in England, who will win the battle – Harold or William?
2 What effect will there be on the English language?

Read Chapters 4 and 5, then answer these questions.

1 What did the king have built after the Battle of Hastings?
2 Which English king lost Normandy to the French?
3 Why did almost a third of the people in England die between 1348 and 1375?
4 Which languages were used for official government papers for two hundred years after 1066?
5 What did John Wycliffe do between 1380 and 1384?
6 What is Geoffrey Chaucer's best-known work?
7 What did William Caxton bring to England in 1476?

Read Chapters 6 and 7, then complete the sentences with the correct names.

King Charles the First / King James the Second / Samuel Johnson / Isaac Newton / William Shakespeare / Jonathan Swift

1 _____ wrote a book in Latin, but later chose English.

2 _____ had the largest vocabulary of any English writer.

3 After _____ was killed, England was without a king for eleven years.

4 _____ was so unpopular that he had to leave England, and his daughter became queen.

5 _____ wanted to fix the English language because he didn't like the continual changes.

6 _____ wrote a dictionary which was a great success.

Read Chapter 8. When were these words introduced?

airport, bronchitis, disco, e-mail, google, nylon, photo, TV

1814: _____	1860: _____
1919: _____	1938: _____
1948: _____	1964: _____
1982: _____	1999: _____

Read Chapter 9. Are these sentences true (T) or false (F)?

1 The English people who settled in Jamestown were the first Europeans to visit America.

2 By 1865 there were millions of Irish slaves in America.

3 Some English people were sent to America as a punishment.

4 The name *Mississippi* comes from Spanish.

5 Before 1664, New York was called New Amsterdam.

6 In American English, *fall* means *winter*.

7 *Fast food* is an American expression which is also used in British English.

Read Chapters 10 and 11, then match these halves of sentences.

1 *Thee* and *thou* are used in some British dialects, but . . .
2 Gaelic is an old Celtic language which . . .
3 The English of Canada is similar to . . .
4 'Spanglish' is a variety of English which . . .
5 Jargon is the special language . . .
6 Some people use slang . . .
7 *Joke* used to be a slang word, but . . .
8 *Grub* and *tucker* are . . .

a slang words for food.
b uses English and Spanish words together.
c it's now part of Standard British English.
d both American and British English.
e is still spoken in the west of Ireland.
f used by people who have the same job or hobby.
g they are not used in Standard British English.
h to show that they belong to a group.

Read Chapter 12, then fill in the gaps with these words.

borrowing, fashionable, foreign, half, harmful, laws, popular, richest, survive, worried

Some people think that over _____ the people in the world
will be able to speak English by 2050. They think that the US
will remain the _____ country in the world, and American
_____ music and films will continue to be _____. But
in some countries people think that it is _____ to teach
children English, because they are _____ that their own
languages might not _____. Some governments want to stop
the _____ of English words, and they have passed _____
against the use of _____ words in some situations.

ACTIVITIES

After Reading

1 **Who's who in the book? Match each person to three of the notes, and join the information together to make five short paragraphs, one about each person.**

King Alfred / Geoffrey Chaucer / James Murray /
Noah Webster / William the Conqueror

1 both a poet and a government official / lived in London
2 a Scotsman / worked on the first Oxford English Dictionary
3 an American teacher / proud of American English
4 leader of Normandy / defeated Harold in 1066 / became king of England
5 a king of Wessex / an important battle against the Vikings
6 planned to finish in ten years / after five years had only reached the word 'ant'
7 wanted to bring back the centres of learning / destroyed by the Vikings
8 wrote a book on spelling / extremely successful
9 wrote in the East Midlands dialect / used words from French
10 took land from rich English families / gave it to his followers
11 spoke French / French became the language of government and business in England
12 died in 1915 / working on the letter U
13 good at describing people / many other writers copied him
14 suggested new spellings / now accepted American spellings
15 decided to make English the language of education / learnt Latin / could translate important books into English

2 **Match the words on the left with the types of language on the right. What do the words mean?**

1 freeway	a Anglo-Saxon dialect
2 unputdownable	b Old English
3 say again	c northern English dialect
4 butty	d Scots
5 y r u L8?	e Modern English
6 lass	f Irish English
7 wealas	g American English
8 div	h Seaspeak
9 clomb	i British slang
10 youse	j text message

3 **Use the words below to complete this paragraph about changes in the English language.**

borrowed, centuries, complain, continually, controlled, developed, expressions, invaders, made, putting, quarter, room, settled, technology, vocabulary

The English language _____ from the dialects spoken by
_____ from northern Europe who _____ in Britain
fifteen _____ ago. Since then, the language has changed
_____. English people have _____ words (like *coffee*)
from other languages, and have _____ new words (like
fingerprint) by _____ old words together. Developments
in _____ have brought new _____, too, like *website*
and *chat* _____ . People often _____ about new words
and _____. But the English language is used by a _____
of the world's people. It can't be _____!

4 **How do you think the use of English will change in the future? Write a report about English in your country in 2050. Use these questions to help you.**

- Will more or fewer people speak English? Why?
- Will English be taught in schools?
- Will English be popular with Internet users?
- Will other languages be more important than English?
- Which languages will people use for business?

5 **Do you agree or disagree with these sentences? Why?**

1 Everyone should learn more than one language.
2 Learning to speak is more important than learning to write.
3 People who live in the same country should speak the same language.
4 If a language is used by very few people, it's important to keep it alive.

6 **Working on your own or in a group, make a list of the English words and expressions that you hear or read in a typical day. Write notes about each word or expression:**

1 What kind of language is it? Do you think it is slang or standard English?
2 Where has it come from? The US or Britain? The Internet, TV or music?
3 Is there an equivalent word or expression in your language?

7 **Explore these websites. See if you can find help with spelling and pronunciation; information about English idioms; and games, tests and quizzes.**

www.askoxford.com
www.britishcouncil.org/learnenglish.htm
www.usingenglish.com

ABOUT THE AUTHOR

Brigit Viney lives in the east of England in the university city of Cambridge. She has lived mainly in Britain, but has also spent a few years in the Middle East, in Syria and Egypt, which she thoroughly enjoyed.

She has worked in English Language Teaching for more than twenty-five years, first as a teacher in Egypt, and then as an editor and writer. She has written grammar practice materials, readers, a course book for children, and teacher's resource books.

She loves travelling to different countries, exploring new cities, eating new food and trying to learn a little of the language. Sometimes the sounds are just too hard to pronounce, however (Czech has some difficult ones!).

Brigit likes cycling round Cambridge, visiting old houses and other historical places, and walking in the country. She likes meals out with friends, trips to the cinema, and art exhibitions. She likes many kinds of art, old and modern, and enjoys drawing and painting, especially landscapes.

OXFORD BOOKWORMS LIBRARY

Classics • Crime & Mystery • Factfiles • Fantasy & Horror
Human Interest • Playscripts • Thriller & Adventure
True Stories • World Stories

The OXFORD BOOKWORMS LIBRARY provides enjoyable reading in English, with a wide range of classic and modern fiction, non-fiction, and plays. It includes original and adapted texts in seven carefully graded language stages, which take learners from beginner to advanced level. An overview is given on the next pages.

All Stage 1 titles are available as audio recordings, as well as over eighty other titles from Starter to Stage 6. All Starters and many titles at Stages 1 to 4 are specially recommended for younger learners. Every Bookworm is illustrated, and Starters and Factfiles have full-colour illustrations.

The OXFORD BOOKWORMS LIBRARY also offers extensive support. Each book contains an introduction to the story, notes about the author, a glossary, and activities. Additional resources include tests and worksheets, and answers for these and for the activities in the books. There is advice on running a class library, using audio recordings, and the many ways of using Oxford Bookworms in reading programmes. Resource materials are available on the website <www.oup.com/elt/bookworms>.

The *Oxford Bookworms Collection* is a series for advanced learners. It consists of volumes of short stories by well-known authors, both classic and modern. Texts are not abridged or adapted in any way, but carefully selected to be accessible to the advanced student.

You can find details and a full list of titles in the *Oxford Bookworms Library Catalogue* and *Oxford English Language Teaching Catalogues*, and on the website <www.oup.com/elt/bookworms>.

THE OXFORD BOOKWORMS LIBRARY
GRADING AND SAMPLE EXTRACTS

STARTER • 250 HEADWORDS
present simple – present continuous – imperative –
can/cannot, must – *going to* (future) – simple gerunds …

Her phone is ringing – but where is it?

Sally gets out of bed and looks in her bag. No phone.
She looks under the bed. No phone. Then she looks behind
the door. There is her phone. Sally picks up her phone and
answers it. *Sally's Phone*

STAGE 1 • 400 HEADWORDS
… past simple – coordination with *and*, *but*, *or* –
subordination with *before*, *after*, *when*, *because*, *so* …

I knew him in Persia. He was a famous builder and I
worked with him there. For a time I was his friend, but
not for long. When he came to Paris, I came after him –
I wanted to watch him. He was a very clever, very dangerous
man. *The Phantom of the Opera*

STAGE 2 • 700 HEADWORDS
… present perfect – *will* (future) – *(don't) have to, must not, could* –
comparison of adjectives – simple *if* clauses – past continuous –
tag questions – *ask/tell* + infinitive …

While I was writing these words in my diary, I decided
what to do. I must try to escape. I shall try to get down the
wall outside. The window is high above the ground, but
I have to try. I shall take some of the gold with me – if I
escape, perhaps it will be helpful later. *Dracula*

STAGE 3 • 1000 HEADWORDS

... should, may – present perfect continuous – *used to* – past perfect
– causative – relative clauses – indirect statements ...

Of course, it was most important that no one should see
Colin, Mary, or Dickon entering the secret garden. So Colin
gave orders to the gardeners that they must all keep away
from that part of the garden in future. ***The Secret Garden***

STAGE 4 • 1400 HEADWORDS

*... past perfect continuous – passive (simple forms) –
would* conditional clauses – indirect questions –
relatives with *where/when* – gerunds after prepositions/phrases ...

I was glad. Now Hyde could not show his face to the world
again. If he did, every honest man in London would be proud
to report him to the police. ***Dr Jekyll and Mr Hyde***

STAGE 5 • 1800 HEADWORDS

*... future continuous – future perfect –
passive (modals, continuous forms) –
would have* conditional clauses – modals + perfect infinitive ...

If he had spoken Estella's name, I would have hit him. I was so
angry with him, and so depressed about my future, that I could
not eat the breakfast. Instead I went straight to the old house.
Great Expectations

STAGE 6 • 2500 HEADWORDS

... passive (infinitives, gerunds) – advanced modal meanings –
clauses of concession, condition

When I stepped up to the piano, I was confident. It was as if I
knew that the prodigy side of me really did exist. And when I
started to play, I was so caught up in how lovely I looked that
I didn't worry how I would sound. ***The Joy Luck Club***

BOOKWORMS · FACTFILES · STAGE 4
Great Crimes
JOHN ESCOTT

It is more than forty years since the Great Train Robbery. Some of the robbers are dead, and only one – Ronnie Biggs – is still in prison. But there is still one thing that the police would like to know: what happened to the rest of the money that was taken? Two million pounds has never been found. Perhaps some of the robbers would like to know the answer to this question too . . .

Many great crimes end in a question. Who really killed President Kennedy? What happened to Shergar? Who knows the truth about Azaria Chamberlain? Not all the answers are known. Join the world's detectives and discover the love, hate, death, money, and mystery held in the stories of these great crimes.

BOOKWORMS · FACTFILES · STAGE 4
Nelson Mandela
ROWENA AKINYEMI

In 1918 in the peaceful province of Transkei, South Africa, the Mandela family gave their new baby son the name Rolihlahla – 'troublemaker'. But the young boy's early years were happy ones, and he grew up to be a good student and an enthusiastic sportsman.

Who could imagine then what was waiting for Nelson Mandela – the tireless struggle for human rights, the long years in prison, the happiness and sadness of family life, and one day the title of President of South Africa? This is the story of an extraordinary man, recognized today as one of the world's great leaders, whose long walk to freedom brought new hope to a troubled nation.